Lerner SPORTS

EXTREME SPEED

SUPERFAST STOCK CAR RACING

Beth Bence Reinke

Lerner Publications ◆ Minneapolis

SCORE BIG with sports fans, reluctant readers, and report writers!

Lerner Sports is a database of high-interest biographies profiling notable sports superstars. Packed with fascinating facts, these bios explore the backgrounds, career-defining moments, and everyday lives of popular athletes. Lerner Sports is perfect for young readers developing research skills or looking for exciting sports content.

LERNER SPORTS FEATURES:
- Keyword search
- Topic navigation menus
- Fast facts
- Related bio suggestions to encourage more reading
- Admin view of reader statistics
- Fresh content updated regularly

and more!

Visit LernerSports.com for a free trial!

Lerner SPORTS

Copyright © 2020 by Lerner Publishing Group, Inc.

All rights reserved. International copyright secured. No part of this book may be reproduced, stored in a retrieval system, or transmitted in any form or by any means—electronic, mechanical, photocopying, recording, or otherwise—without the prior written permission of Lerner Publishing Group, Inc., except for the inclusion of brief quotations in an acknowledged review.

CONTENTS

CHAPTER 1
NASCAR'S ROOTS 4

CHAPTER 2
THE RACING MACHINE 10

CHAPTER 3
THE CREW BEHIND THE CAR 18

CHAPTER 4
IT'S RACE DAY! 24

STOCK CAR FAMILY TREE 29
GLOSSARY 30
FURTHER INFORMATION 31
INDEX 32

CHAPTER 1
NASCAR'S ROOTS

Stock cars zoom around the track at the Daytona 500.

It was the last lap of the 2016 Daytona 500. Denny Hamlin and Martin Truex Jr. zoomed around the final turn side by side. As the cars raced to the checkered flag, fans in the grandstands jumped to their feet to get a closer look. Both cars zoomed across the finish line, but it was hard to tell which car crossed the line first.

4

FACTS AT A GLANCE

- A stock car weighs more than 3,300 pounds (1,500 kg).

- Stock cars travel up to 200 miles (320 km) per hour.

- NASCAR races take an entire weekend. Race teams travel to the track on Thursday. On Friday and Saturday, drivers and **pit crews** practice. The actual race is on Sunday afternoon.

- **NASCAR Cup Series** teams use up to thirteen sets of tires every race weekend. The tires are smooth and wide, which helps them grip the track. If a tire goes flat, an inner liner keeps the car from scraping on the track.

The results came in. The nose of Hamlin's stock car was ahead. He won by one hundredth of a second. It was the closest finish in Daytona 500 history.

Hamlin's car was just barely ahead of Truex Jr.'s car when they crossed the finish line in 2016.

The greatest stock car drivers are featured in the NASCAR Hall of Fame in Charlotte, North Carolina.

Stock car racing began in the southeastern United States. Drivers bought cars from the stock, or available cars, at a car dealership. This is where stock car racing gets its name.

Early races were informally organized. In 1947, the National Association for Stock Car Auto Racing (NASCAR) was formed. It oversees every race to make sure things go smoothly.

In the 1950s, Richard Petty began racing. Petty holds the record for the most NASCAR Cup Series race wins with 200. His nickname is "The King." Petty owns a NASCAR race team today.

Petty won the NASCAR Cup championship seven times. Only two other drivers in history have won seven Cup championships—Dale Earnhardt Sr. and Jimmie Johnson.

Richard Petty *(left)* is a record-holding stock car racer. His career spanned forty years.

The NASCAR season has thirty-six races from February to November. Each race is about 3 or 4 hours long. Millions of loyal fans watch on television and at the track.

It's easy to get hooked on NASCAR racing. Stock cars race inches apart and travel at high speeds. It's thrilling to watch!

Martin Truex Jr. won the Toyota Owners 400 in April 2019.

CHAPTER 2
THE RACING MACHINE

Stock cars are more powerful than the cars that people normally drive.

10

Race cars are built for safety and speed.

Building a race car isn't cheap. Each vehicle costs about $200,000. First, the car's steel skeleton is welded together. It includes the **chassis** and **roll cage**. Then, **fabricators** shape the body of the car. Many other parts are added to the car, such as the **fuel cell**. The fuel cell holds almost 18 gallons (68 L) of fuel that powers the engine.

> Stock cars use air flow to cool down the engine. This prevents the engine from catching on fire.

NASCAR rules make sure that all race cars are built in similar ways. A stock car weighs more than 3,300 pounds (1,500 kg). Each car is weighed and inspected before it can race. This helps NASCAR make sure the teams are following the rules.

With its powerful engine, a stock car can go 200 miles (320 km) per hour. However, the engine gets extremely hot during races. So stock cars have an air intake in the front of the car. Air flows in to help cool the engine. Sometimes a piece of **debris** such as a candy wrapper gets stuck there. If debris blocks the air too long, the engine will overheat.

REALLY?!

Each car in NASCAR has its own number and colorful paint scheme. However, the paint scheme does not include any actual paint! Instead, stock cars are wrapped with giant stickers made out of vinyl material. These stickers may include logos for businesses that sponsor the race car team. Even the headlights are stickers.

Each race car seat is custom made to fit the driver's body. This special seat helps keep the driver safe during a wreck. The driver wears a HANS device too. HANS stands for Head and Neck Support. The device keeps the driver's head from jerking forward or sideways during a crash.

Stock cars have other safety features to protect the driver. Roof flaps pop up when a car spins. Air hitting the flaps stops the car from flying high into the air during a crash.

HANS devices protect drivers' heads and necks if their cars crash during the race.

Crashes during NASCAR races can be very dangerous.

Sometimes a stock car rolls over during a crash. The steel roll cage keeps the driver from being crushed. Additionally, windshields are made of shatterproof plastic. If the windshield breaks during a crash, it won't break into sharp pieces.

15

NASCAR driver Joey Logano climbs through his car window at Bristol Motor Speedway in 2016.

Cars often hit the wall of the track during races. The impact can be painful for the driver. Thick foam padding inside the driver's door absorbs energy so it doesn't hurt the driver as much.

Doors on stock cars do not open. Drivers climb in the car through the window. The windows have no glass. Instead, a safety net keeps the driver's arms inside the car during a wreck.

Even the tires help with safety. NASCAR tires are smooth and wide. This base helps them grip the track. There's a second, smaller tire inside called the inner liner. If a tire goes flat, the inner liner buoys the car body so it doesn't scrape against the track on the way to the **pit box**. A set of four racing tires costs about $1,800. NASCAR Cup Series teams use up to thirteen sets of tires every race weekend. That's expensive rubber!

Crew members inspect NASCAR tires before every race.

CHAPTER 3
THE CREW BEHIND THE CAR

Team haulers transport the cars and other gear to each race track.

At the beginning of the race week, engineers and mechanics get the race car ready. The **crew chief** oversees their work.

The pit crew practices for race day. It repairs and refuels the stock cars. The crew practices pit stops over and over. They jack up the car, change the tires, and put in fuel. Every move must be fast and exact.

Race teams travel to the track on Thursday. The team hauler gets there first. A hauler is a huge truck with a long, tall trailer. The hauler transports gear, cars, and the race team. Each hauler serves as a home base for its crew.

Drivers are busy on Friday and Saturday. They run qualifying laps. Cars with the fastest lap times start at the front on race day.

Members of the pit crew sit in the war wagon to monitor the racer during each lap.

Crews in the garage are working too. Mechanics repair cars between laps. Tire specialists manage dozens of tires.

On Sunday morning, teams organize their pit boxes for race day. Each pit box has two sections. One is a parking spot. The other is an area behind the pit wall. That's where the pit crew sets up the war wagon. The war wagon is a giant toolbox filled with tools and car parts. It has TVs, computers, and cameras for the crew chief and team engineer to use. They sit atop the war wagon during the race.

Pit crew members stay in their pit box. When the car comes in for a pit stop, they move fast. They have specific jobs. Some refuel the car. Others change the tires.

During a race, pit crew members repair the car as quickly as possible.

One crew member is not in the pit box. The spotter stands high above the track wearing a headset. He talks to the driver during the race. The spotter helps the driver pass other cars and avoid wrecks.

Wrecks still happen though. Sometimes the cars even catch on fire. That's why drivers and pit crew members wear fireproof suits and gloves. They have helmets and protective shoes too. The gas person also wears a special apron to shield her from fuel spills. Working on a NASCAR pit crew is dangerous. But many crew members believe that it is fun too!

Stock cars can catch on fire during crashes. Drivers protect themselves using fireproof suits.

PROFILE IN SPEED

JIMMIE JOHNSON. Jimmie Johnson started racing motorcycles when he was five years old. He now races stock cars in NASCAR races. Johnson also works with charities that help kids in need and give money to schools for special projects.

In 2019, Johnson was the most accomplished of all the NASCAR stars who were still driving. He is a seven-time champion, tied with Petty and Earnhardt.

CHAPTER 4
IT'S RACE DAY!

The Daytona 500 attracts large crowds of people who watch from the grandstand.

The official NASCAR season starts with its most famous race: the Daytona 500. At the first Daytona 500 in 1948, the cars actually raced on the sand at Daytona Beach in Florida. The race moved to the Daytona International Speedway in 1959. Many fans today tune in to watch the race on television. In 2019, approximately 9.1 million people watched the Daytona 500.

The Brickyard 400 is another well-known race. It's run at Indianapolis Motor Speedway in Indiana. A path of bricks marks the start-finish line. These bricks are from the original speedway, which was built in 1909. In 1996, NASCAR racer Dale Jarrett leaned down and kissed the bricks after he won the race. The rest of his team joined him. "Kissing the bricks" soon became a tradition for NASCAR race winners at the speedway.

REALLY?!

Race day is exciting. Famous bands play live concerts. T-shirts and caps are for sale. Drivers meet with fans to take selfies or sign autographs. Fans with special passes can visit the garage to see the cars up close. At some races, fans can even walk on the track before the race.

On race morning, drivers can hang out with their families. Around lunchtime, drivers attend a meeting. Then they put on their fire suits and head to pit road.

Soon, the opening ceremonies begin. Drivers and crews line up on pit road. A pastor prays, and a singer performs the national anthem. On the last note, everyone looks skyward for the military flyover.

Then, everyone gets down to business. Drivers strap in and put in their radio earpieces. They pull on their helmets and gloves. A crew member puts up the window net.

An announcer speaks into a microphone: "Drivers, start your engines!" Each driver flips a switch inside the cockpit. Forty engines roar to life. The racers drive off pit road onto the track. When the green flag waves, the race is on!

For the next few hours, the drivers go fast. Fans watch cars zoom by in a blur of colors. The smell of hot tires and engines drifts through the air.

Pit road is full of action on race day.

Drivers talk to their crew chiefs and spotters over the team radio. When cars come to pit road, pit crews spring into action. They put on four new tires and fuel the car in about 15 seconds.

When the white flag flies, it means there's one lap to go. Whoever crosses the finish line first wins. The winning driver and team go to **Victory Lane**.

In the future, stock cars may change shape. They may get more powerful engines. They may even run on electricity instead of fuel. But no matter what, NASCAR will continue to thrill fans for years to come.

The entire team celebrates a win at the end of the race.

STOCK CAR
FAMILY TREE

NASCAR stock cars have changed over the past 70 years. But one thing has always stayed the same—they're made to go fast!

Hudson Hornet, 1950s

Plymouth Superbird, 1970s

Ford Thunderbird, 1990s

Toyota Camry, 2010s

GLOSSARY

chassis
the body of the car that other parts attach to

crew chief
the leader of the race team who oversees the car and crew

debris
trash and other particles that may get stuck in the air vents during a race

fabricators
workers who build machines

fuel cell
the gas tank in a race car

NASCAR Cup Series
the highest level of stock car racing

pit box
a space on pit road where crew members service the car during the race

pit crew
the five-member team that services the car during a NASCAR race

roll cage
a framework of steel tubing surrounding the driver

Victory Lane
the special area at a race track where a driver and team go to celebrate their win

FURTHER INFORMATION

Acceleration Nation
http://accelerationnation.com

Fishman, Jon M. *Cool Stock Cars*. Minneapolis: Lerner Publications, 2019.

NASCAR
http://www.nascar.com

Reinke, Beth Bence. *Behind the Wheel of a Stock Car*. North Mankato, MN: Childs World, 2016.

Rule, Heather. *Ultimate NASCAR Road Trip*. Minneapolis: Abdo Publishing, 2018.

Savage, Jeff. *Auto Racing Super Stats*. Minneapolis: Lerner Publications, 2017.

INDEX

engine, 11, 13, 27, 28

HANS device, 14
hauler, 19

Johnson, Jimmie, 8, 23

National Association for Stock Car Auto Racing (NASCAR), 5, 7, 8, 9, 12, 13, 17, 22, 25, 28

paint scheme, 13
Petty, Richard, 8, 23
pit crew, 5, 19, 20, 21, 22, 28

safety, 14, 15, 16, 17
skeleton, 11
spotter, 22, 28

tires, 5, 17, 19, 20, 21, 27, 28

wreck, 14–15, 17, 22

PHOTO ACKNOWLEDGMENTS

The images in this book are used with the permission of: © Action Sports Photography/Shutterstock.com, pp. 4, 8, 9, 10, 11, 15, 21, 22, 28; © action sports/Shutterstock.com, pp. 5, 14, 17, 27; © Stephen Arce/Icon Sportswire/Corbis/Getty Images, p. 6; © meunierd/Shutterstock.com, p. 7; © Richard Thornton/Shutterstock.com, 12; © Matt Sullivan/Getty Images Sport/Getty Images, p. 16; © Jared C. Tilton/NASCAR/Getty Images, p. 18; © Warren Wimmer/Icon SMI/Newscom, p. 20; © Sean Gardner/Getty Images Sport/Getty Images, p. 23; © Chris Trotman/NASCAR/Getty Images, p. 24; © Roman Korotkov/Shutterstock.com, p. 29 (top left); © The Enthusiast Network/Getty Images, p. 29 (top right); © Brian Cleary/Getty Images Sport/Getty Images, p. 29 (bottom left); © Gregory Fisher/Icon Sportswire/Getty Images, p. 29 (bottom right).

Front Cover: © Action Sports Photography/Shutterstock.com.